One summer morning deep in the nest,

a brand-new honeybee
　　squirms,
　　　　pushes,
　　　　　chews
through the wax cap of her solitary cell and into . . .
a teeming, trembling flurry.
Hummmmm!

CANDACE FLEMING   ERIC ROHMANN

HONEYBEE

THE BUSY LIFE OF *APIS MELLIFERA*

NEAL PORTER BOOKS

HOLIDAY HOUSE/NEW YORK

Tongues lick.
Antennae touch.
Bodies clamber and scramble over thin wax comb.
The new bee rests.
Soft, fuzzy, and female—like all newly emerged worker bees—
her scientific name is *Apis mellifera*,
or *Apis* for short.

Crawling to a cell packed with sticky, rich pollen,
Apis eats.
    And eats.
        And eats some more.
Her wings dry. Her color
darkens to a warm yellow orange.
Her muscles grow strong.

Strong enough for flying?

Not yet . . . cleaning comes first.
Apis's first job is to tidy the hive's nursery.
She hauls away leftover bits,
    carts off old wax caps,
        leaves each cell ready for a new bee egg.
When she turns three days old, special glands
behind her face swell and expand.
Soon she is ready for her next job.

Flying?

Not yet . . . nursing.
The grub-like larvae get all her attention.
She checks them.
   Inspects them.
Feeds them a milky-sweet
liquid made with those glands.

On Apis's eighth day of life,
she leaves the nursery.

For flying?

Not yet . . . queen tending.
Long and graceful, the queen glides across the combs.
Two thousand times a day—the queen stops to drop
a single egg into a single cell.
        Pearly white.
                Half the size of a grain of rice.
                        Each will grow into a bee.
The queen doesn't have time to take care of herself.
So Apis and the others groom her with their forelegs,
        examine her with their tongues,
                feed her a drop of sweet brood food,
                        worker mouth to queen mouth.
As they do, they pick up the queen's scent
        with their antennae,
                legs,
                        tongues.
They pass this scent along to the rest of the nest . . .
a message that the queen is healthy and safe.

When Apis turns twelve days old, glands in her
abdomen begin making flakes of white wax.
It is time for her new job.

Flying?

Not yet . . . comb building.
Using her wax, her sharp, spoon-shaped jaws, and her legs, she
shapes,
   molds,
     maneuvers
       to create cells.

But Apis is not a builder for long. Three days later, she starts . . .

Flying?

Not yet . . . food handling.

Apis stands on soft honeycomb, waiting.

A forager bee approaches. Dusted with pollen and smelling
of sunshine and fresh air, she is loaded with nectar.

Food for the colony!

Apis creeps toward her.

Furry heads bump.

And the forager brings up the nectar into her open mouth.

Sticking out her straw-like tongue, Apis sips up the nectar.

   She folds and unfolds,

      folds and unfolds,

         folds and unfolds her mouth.

Until the nectar grows

   thicker,

      stickier.

She stores the half-dried nectar in an empty cell. Over the
next few days it will ripen into honey.

When Apis turns eighteen days old, she is ready to start her
life *outside*.

Flying?

Not yet . . . guarding.

    Against birds.

        Or bears.

            And bees from other nests.

Patrolling a tiny patch by the hive's entrance, Apis sniffs each incoming worker with her antennae.

Friend or foe?

Two bees hover nearby.

Apis bends her antennae toward them and tests the air.

They do not smell like members of her colony.

She stands on her hind legs.

They do not act like colony members.

Apis lets off an alarm scent to warn the others.

Robber bees!

They've come to steal honey from the nest.

Apis flings herself at one of them.

The two grab hold of each other's legs.

    They curl their abdomens.

        They roll and grapple.

Apis buzzes, bites, burrows.

She is willing to give up her life to protect her nest and its honey.

She bites harder.

Shaking her off, the robber flies away.

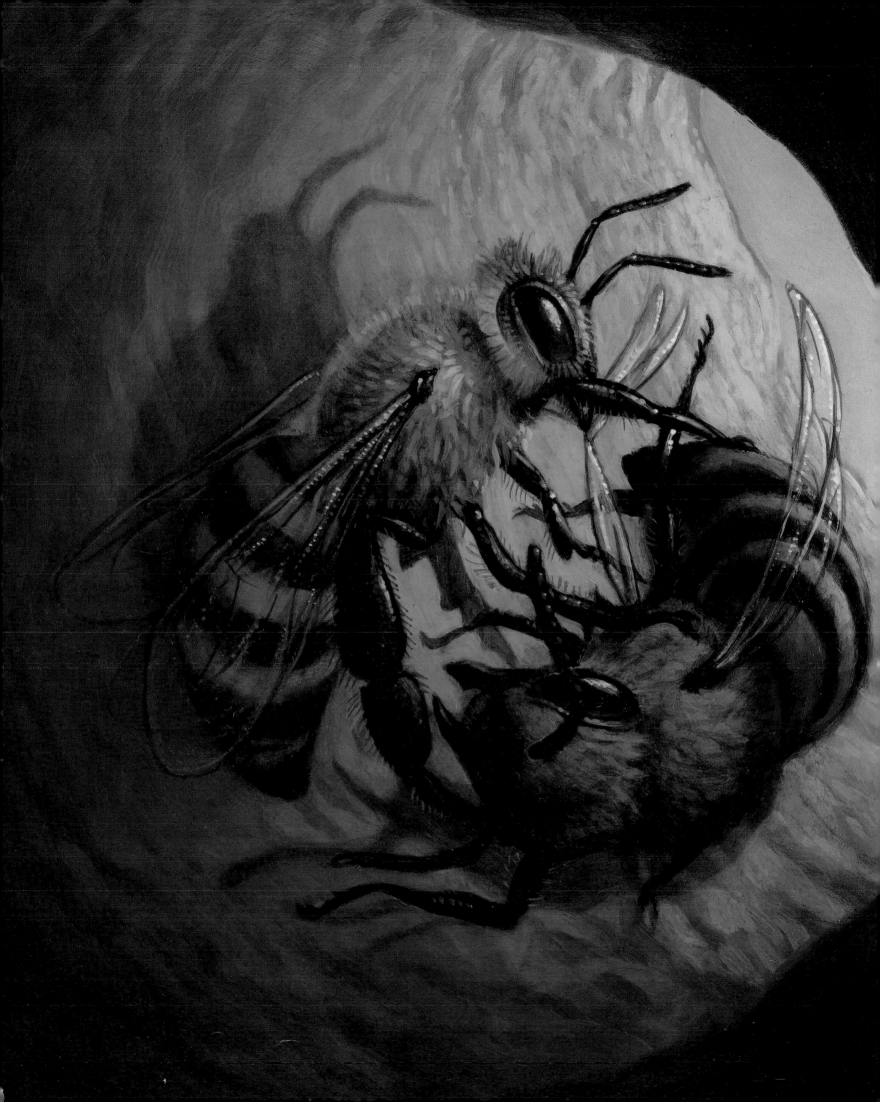

Flies!

At last, on the twenty-fifth day of her life—with
the sun just rising and the dew still drying—
she leaps from the nest and . . .

Thousands of other bees rise from the nest, too,
first to orient themselves and then to forage for
water, or collect a sticky plant sap called
propolis, a kind of bee glue,
or gather pollen.
And Apis?
She is in search of sweet nectar.
Her antennae taste the breeze.

Milkweed.

Coneflower.

Clover.

She can smell the sugary goodness inside
their blossoms.

    Apis follows the floral odor
        for miles,
           wings beating two hundred times a second
           until . . .

She circles down.

     She alights on a blossom.

          She scrabbles over its petals, searching for nectar inside.
Poking her long tongue deep inside the flower,
she sips and swallows,
and skips to the next flower.
The sugary fluid does not go into her belly.
It goes into a special sac called a honey stomach.
This is how Apis will carry her nectar home.
As she visits each flower, grains of pollen stick
to her brushy body.
They cling to her bristly legs.
She carries this pollen
from flower to flower,
     brushing it off,
          picking it up,
               pollinating the field.
At last, her honey stomach weighs almost as
much as she does.
Then, wings working hard,
     she flies
          back to the hive,
where she gives up her nectar to a food handler.

Now will she rest?

No . . . she will dance!
Wagging her tail, Apis circles to the left,
    then to the right.
        She runs in a long, straight line.
Other bees gather around.
They listen to the vibrations of her dance.
Apis is giving directions.
She is telling them the nectar is sweet.
She is asking them to go there, too.
Soon a stream of bees head for her find.
Apis makes nine more trips that day,
    gathering,
        pollinating,
            before the sun finally sets, and she can rest.

But she will go back tomorrow.

And the day after that.

And the day after that.

She grows thinner and slower. She loses her hair.

Her wings fray and tatter.

Summertime bees do not live long.

And Apis is now thirty-five days old.

She has flown back and forth between nest and blossoms,

five hundred miles in all.

She has visited thirty thousand flowers.

She has collected enough nectar to make

one-twelfth of a teaspoon of honey.

Her work is done.

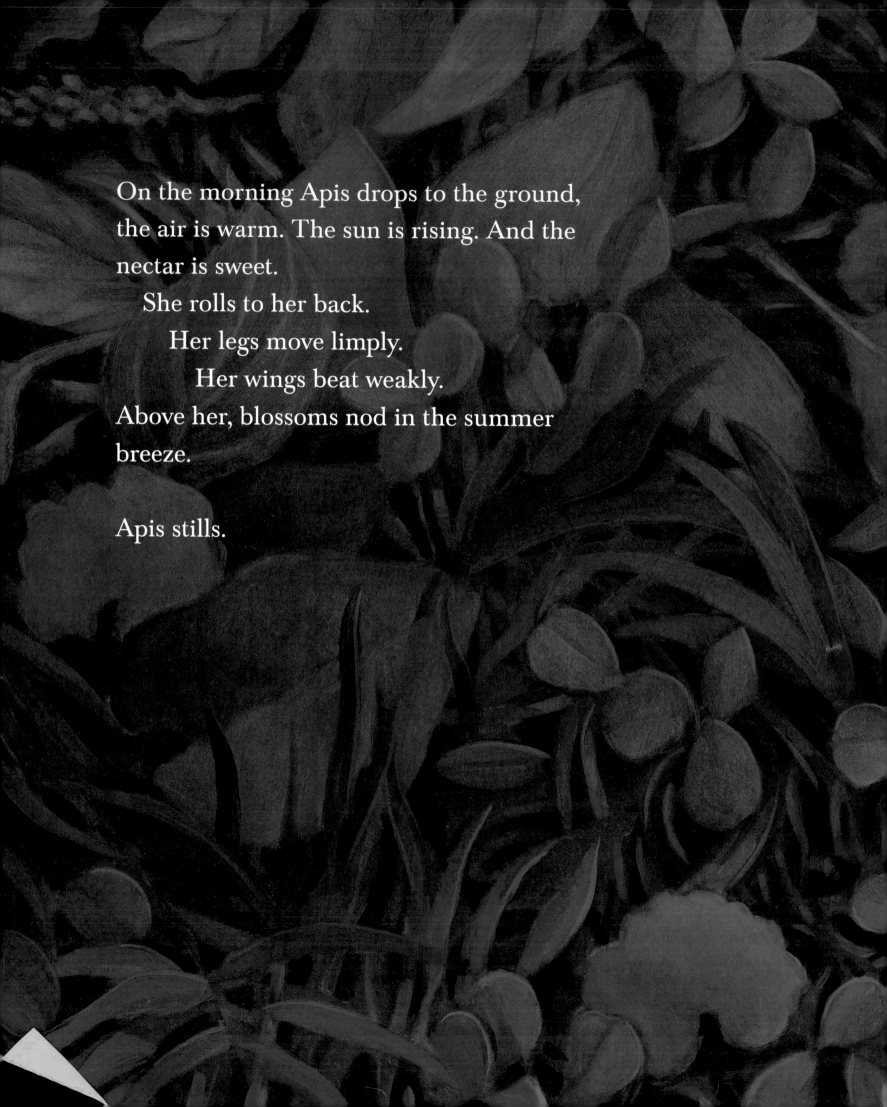

On the morning Apis drops to the ground, the air is warm. The sun is rising. And the nectar is sweet.

She rolls to her back.

Her legs move limply.

Her wings beat weakly.

Above her, blossoms nod in the summer breeze.

Apis stills.

And back in the nest, a brand-new honeybee
squirms,
pushes,
chews
through the wax cap of her solitary cell and into . . .
a teeming, trembling flurry.
Hummmmm!

A worker honeybee's body is made up of three sections: the **head**, a middle section called the **thorax** and a back end called the **abdomen**. Within each of these sections are individual body parts that give *Apis mellifera* her amazing abilities. Here are some of those parts.

WINGS Apis has two pairs of these. The front pair is much bigger than the back pair. A row of hooks on each back pair fits into a groove on the front pair. This holds the wings together, giving Apis a smoother, faster flight.

STINGER The stinger is almost invisible until used. Located inside a special chamber at the very end of Apis's abdomen, the stinger is extended only when she senses danger. As the stinger penetrates skin, venom is pumped from her venom sac, also located in the abdomen. It is this venom that causes the bee sting to hurt. Bees can only sting humans and other mammals once—stinging kills the bee.

LEGS Apis has three pairs of legs. Her forelegs have hairy brushes on them used to remove dust, dirt and pollen from her head, as well as an "antennae cleaner" through which her antennae can be pulled and swept clean. The middle legs are used to remove pollen that has accumulated on the thorax, which is then pushed back to the hind legs. They pack it into the **pollen baskets**. The pollen baskets are located on the outside of the hind legs—one on the right, one on the left. When the baskets are full, Apis returns to the hive. With her middle legs she removes the pollen from her baskets and passes it to another worker who stores it by pressing it into an empty cell.

EYES Apis has five of these! Her two big eyes (called compound eyes) take up most of her head and are used to distinguish light and color, making them especially useful for spying flowers. Her three tiny eyes, called ocelli, are too small to be seen here. They are arranged in a triangular pattern between her compound eyes. They have just one purpose—determining the brightness and intensity of light.

ANTENNAE The antennae, located on either side of Apis's triangle-shaped head, are her nose. Swiveling in all directions, they pick up thousands of scents, including flowers and the chemicals (called pheromones) that transmit messages in the hive. Super-sensitive, the antennae can also detect the nest's temperature, as well as its humidity level. What's more, Apis uses her antennae to guide her as she moves inside the dark hive, for taste, and for measuring her flight speed.

PROBOSCIS This long, straw-like organ has many functions. It can be used to reach into flowers and suck up nectar, as well as to ingest water and honey. Additionally, it is used to exchange food between worker bees, as well as between workers and the queen. And it is used for communication. After licking pheromones from the queen, workers pass them on to others.

MANDIBLES These powerful, spoon-shaped jaws have lots of uses, including cutting, shaping, and maneuvering wax for hive construction; dragging dead bees and other debris out of the nest; grooming; fighting; and holding on to surfaces.

HELPING OUT HONEYBEES

Most people sitting down to dinner don't realize the important role honeybees played in preparing that meal. Here's a surprising fact: one out of every three mouthfuls of food in the American diet is, in some way, a product of honeybee pollination—from fruits to nuts to vegetables.

No wonder beekeepers were alarmed when, in 2006, they noticed a strange phenomenon. Huge numbers of adult worker honeybees were abandoning their colonies, leaving behind queens, immature bees, and hives full of honey and pollen. What was driving them away? No one knew. But the effects were dire. The disappearance of these bees led to the collapse of colonies—both wild and domestic—all over the world.

The good news is that the number of reported cases of "colony collapse disorder" has decreased in the last five years. The bad news is that bee populations continue to decline. Why are there fewer bees around?

There is no single cause. Instead, scientists believe it is a combination of many factors, including the use of pesticides, climate change, disease, and loss of habitat. As scientists continue to investigate these and other possible causes of declining bee populations, some experts are looking for ways to help plants survive without bees. In Japan, for example, researchers have developed insect-sized drones called "bee-bots" capable of artificial pollination. Covered with a patch of horsehair bristles, these tiny robots can collect and transfer pollen from one plant to another.

Even with an army of pollinating robots, however, farmers would face lots of problems. That's because there are 20,000 species of bees in the world, each with unique flight patterns and body sizes to get into different flowers. Bumblebees, for example, are the best pollinators for blueberries and tomatoes, while leaf-cutter bees are best for alfalfa. It is this diversity of bees and flight patterns that lead to efficient and effective pollination. That's why scientists and beekeepers say it makes more sense to protect honeybees and other natural pollinators.

How can we help? First, we can provide pesticide-free habitats with lots of flowers. Bee-friendly plants are easy to grow. Scatter a variety throughout your yard or in your container garden. A few pointers: Bees prefer yellow, blue, and purple flowers. Clover is a good choice. So is coneflower. Other plants bees love are sage, lavender, bee balm, and heather.

We can also give bees a voice by writing to our congressmen and senators, urging them to not only support funding for honeybee research, but to spend money on habitat enhancements.

And last, because we rely on domestic honeybees to pollinate our crops and gardens, we should seek out local beekeepers and buy their honey. Keeping them in business is good for everyone—bees and people.

A BIT MORE BUZZ

1. Bees are the only insects in the world that make food people can eat . . . honey!

2. A colony can contain between 20,000 and 60,000 bees.

3. Members of a colony are divided into three groups:

Queen—A colony has a single queen. Despite her royal title, the queen does not rule the colony. Her job is to lay the eggs that spawn the nest's next generation of bees. Commonly living two to three years, during the summer (the queen's busiest season) she can lay 2,000 eggs a day. She also produces chemicals that guide the behavior of other bees.

Workers—All female, the workers take on the nest's chores, from cleaning to foraging. Workers are the only bees most people ever see flying around outside.

Drones—These are the male bees and their sole purpose is to mate with the queen. They have no stinger and they do no other work. They don't even feed themselves. A worker does that for them. During the spring and summer months, several hundred drones live in the nest. But when winter comes and the nest goes into survival mode, the drones are chased out.

4. It takes twenty-one days for a worker bee to grow. It starts with the queen, who lays a tiny egg at the bottom of a cell in the comb. In three days, a grub-like creature called a larva hatches from the egg. The worker bees then feed the larva. It grows bigger each day until it is almost as big as the cell. On the eighth day, the larva spins a cocoon. Inside the cocoon, a pupa develops from the larva. It starts to look more like an insect than a grub. It grows eyes, legs, and wings. On the twenty-first day it sheds its cocoon and chews its way out of the cell. A new worker is born.

5. Most honeybees in the United States are raised commercially by beekeepers in man-made hives. (Wild bee nests are rare due to disease and parasites.) According to the United States Department of Agriculture there are about 212,000 beekeepers tending almost three million colonies, making the United States the world's third largest honey producer.

6. A honeybee's sense of smell is so acute that scientists have been able to train them to sniff out bombs, dead bodies, and other distinct odors.

7. Forager bees tend to specialize in what they collect. Some gather nectar; others collect pollen; still others collect water or propolis, a sticky plant sap used for nest repair. Less than 3% of foraging honeybees have mixed loads.

8. Honeybees pass along information about nectar and pollen to the rest of their nest mates by dancing. There are two kinds:

In the **Round Dance**, the bee circles in one direction, then turns around and circles back in the other direction. Bees use this dance when a food source is nearby. Because food has been found so close, the dance does not show the flower's exact location. Instead, foragers leave the nest and spread out, searching for them.

The **Figure Eight Dance** is an elaborate dance.

First the bee runs in a straight line, waggling its abdomen. Then it turns in one direction and makes a semicircle turn back to the starting point, waggles in another straight line, turns in the other direction and repeats. This dance is followed by potential recruits who learn where and how far away the flowers are located. How? The distance is communicated by the length of the dance's straight, vibrating run, while its direction is gleaned from the angle of the dance on the honeycomb in relation to the sun. The food source's quality is communicated by the intensity of the waggle. Lackluster waggles mean lesser quality and usually recruits fewer foragers while vigorous, enthusiastic waggles can recruit hundreds of bees.

BUZZING AROUND ONLINE

There are plenty of places to find honeybees online. Here are a few of my favorites:

Watch Apis do the waggle dance:
https://video.nationalgeographic.com/video/weirdest-bees-dance

Get an inside look at the hive's queen, drones, and workers.
https://www.sciencekids.co.nz/videos/animals/bees.html

See the stages of a honeybee from egg to adult worker:
https://www.youtube.com/watch?v=f6mJ7e5YmnE

And here's a site chock-full of photos and facts about honeybees. Don't miss the video of a guard bee attacking a robber.
https://kids.nationalgeographic.com/animals/honeybee

MORE BOOKS ABOUT BEES

Florian, Douglas. *UnBEElievables: Honeybee Poems and Paintings.* New York: Beach Lane Books, 2012.

Heligmann, Deborah. *Jump Into Science: Honeybees.* New York: National Geographic Children's Books, reprint, 2017.

Milner, Charlotte. *The Bee Book.* London: DK Children's Publishing, 2018.

Rotner, Shelley and Anne Woodhull. *The Buzz on Bees: Why Are They Disappearing?* New York: Holiday House, 2010.

Slade, Suzanne and Carol Schwartz, ill. *What If There Were No Bees?: A Book About the Grassland Ecosystem.* Mankato, MN: Picture Window Books, 2010.